MW01713430

IMAGES
of America

OTISCO LAKE COMMUNITY

This is a section of an 1878 map from the *History of Onondaga County 1615–1878*. Otisco Lake is shown in its proximity to surrounding towns and landmarks.

The cover of this book shows the Amber Beachmen from the early 1900s. The gentleman sitting on the post is William Gorham of Elbridge, who owned property in Amber.

IMAGES
of America

OTISCO LAKE COMMUNITY

Roger N. Trendowski

ARCADIA

First published 1998

ISBN 0-7524-1269-8

Published by Arcadia Publishing,
an imprint of the Chalford Publishing Corporation,
One Washington Center, Dover, New Hampshire 03820.
Printed in Great Britain

Library of Congress Cataloging-in-Publication Data applied for

Contents

Acknowledgements

The photographs reproduced in this book have come from both the historical societies and private collections of current and past residents of the Otisco Lake area. Each collection by itself was excellent. Images from all the collections complemented the total story of the lake community. To all the contributors to the book, thank you very much. To my mother, Ethel Wheeler Trendowski, I want to extend my deepest thanks because I could not have done it without you.

Editorial Review and Material Contributors: Jack Dillon, Marcellus; Peg Nolan, Marcellus Historical Society; Peter Oster, Amber; Nancy Shelley, Town of Otisco Historian; Barbara Shoemaker, Town of Spafford Historian; Ethel Trendowski, Amber; Cy and Pat Vile, Amber; and Malcolm Wheeler, Amber.

Contributors (pictures, stories, guidance): Connie Amidon, Marcellus; Jane Amidon, Burma Road Historian; Gail Banks, Marietta; Grace Bishop, Otisco Valley Road; Rev. Richard Chaffee, Amber Congregational Church; Ann Dolan, Fitzgerald Point; Jennifer Donovan, Marietta House; Nancy Frost, Amber; Florence Henderson, Amber; Rose Kronen, Amber; Lois Locke, Oak Hill; William Marten, Otisco Valley Road; Bill Reagan, Marcellus Historical Society; Greta Renfro, Skaneateles; Marjorie Seeley, Amber; Teal and Pat Trendowski, Amber; Raymond and Gladys Wheeler, Oak Hill Road; Charley Woeller, Postmaster, Marietta; References from the Syracuse Chapter, National Railway Historical Society (April 1950); References and pictures from *The Herald Journal* Syracuse Newspaper; References and pictures from the Otisco Lake Community Association; and References and pictures from the Amber Congregational Church.

Editing: Patti Carlisle and Carissa Trendowski.

Introduction

Otisco Lake Community provides a visual history of this central New York Finger Lake region and the villages of Amber and Marietta over a 70-year time span (1880s–1950s), with the concentration of photographs covering the period between 1900 to 1935. Two hundred and twenty photographs, postcards, and exhibits have been gathered from local historical societies in Otisco, Spafford, and Marcellus as well as from more than a dozen families who live in the lake area.

The book takes a visual trip around the lakefront in the early 1900s, starting at Fitzgerald Point, Wheeler Terrace, Heath's Grove, Lamb's Grove, Bouttelle inlet, Amber Beach, and down through the "narrows" to the dam. It continues along the west shore past Forest Home and Burma Road properties. The tour concludes with Twin Oaks boarding house and marina and the story of the early "causeway," with pictures showing horse and buggy traffic crossing the lake using this narrow land bridge. The images in *Otisco Lake Community* present a time when people dressed formally even during their recreation; tourists and boarding houses were numerous; and local stores, recreation halls, and picnic grounds were plentiful. The book shows how people of the early 1900s traveled. There are pictures of the M & OL Railway train that transported visitors to the lake, as well as Otisco Lake's largest passenger boat, *Fontney*, which took people to their homes and cottages on the lake. Many individuals, families, and local groups who played key roles in the development of the lake community are identified.

Some photographs from the 1940s and 1950s are also included in this 128-page visual history. This material is necessary to provide readers with a more complete sense of Otisco Lake's community and people. These include photographs of the Amber Fire Department and Amber Congregational Church and an introduction to the Otisco Lake Community Association, which began in the mid-1950s. These organizations have been essential to the development of the lake area.

Historians and even casual readers may find omissions or errors in this book which should be corrected in future editions. Records of the time were not kept well and few people in the community still recall the early 1900s. One of my top priorities in writing this book was to create an awareness of history for the residents and summer visitors to Otisco Lake. I encourage all who have additional photographs, postcards, and stories to contact the local historical societies in Otisco, Spafford, and Marcellus. Working together, we can preserve the history of the people and the area. Also, please tell me what additional photographs and literature you have. My electronic web page is http://home.att.net/~rtrendowski, and my email address is rtrendowski@worldnet.att.net.

Where did Otisco Lake get its name? After researching this question, reading a four-inch Onondaga County history book (1615–1878), and talking to several local historians and residents, the answer is, "no one is absolutely sure." One premise is that the word "Otisco" is a Native American word. The Iroquois Confederation ruled over this area of central New York. One characteristic of the Iroquois language was that one's lips did not come together to form spoken words. Words such as Onondaga, Otisco, and Skaneateles all have this same characteristic. The earliest white settlers on record at Otisco Lake were Oliver Tuttle and his son Daniel. They came from Cincinnatus (now called Cortland county) and made the first land improvement near the "head" of the lake, the south end. Over the next four years, several other families of settlers arrived. Tuttle built the first frame house in 1804. Then, in the period between 1805 and 1820, many additional families began establishing farms, stores, and boarding houses, primarily because of the development of commerce created by the Hamilton & Skaneateles Turnpike. The turnpike followed both Native American and settler wagon trails from Richfield through Brookfield, Hamilton, and Fabius to the outlet of Otisco Lake, then on to the outlet of Skaneateles Lake. This road, laid out in 1806 and built over the next several years, was an important trading route across central New York. Travelers on the turnpike came west down Oak Hill to the lake, turned north through what is now Amber and Marietta, then turned west out of the valley to Borodino, and then on to Skaneateles. Families settling in Amber and the surrounding area in this early 1800s period included the Kenyons, Kinyons, Kinneys, Hillyers, Niles, Bouttelles, Fishs, Cards, Redways, Langworthys, Teffys, Wells, Andomons, and Oldens.

To my wife, Ginna,
Thanks you for your support and patience
While I was writing this book.

One
Otisco Lake Area

Otisco Lake, one of the lakes left in the path of the great glacier that once covered New York state, lies in the Finger Lakes Region. Located southwest of Syracuse and east of Skaneateles Lake, Otisco Lake is approximately six miles long and one mile wide at its widest point. Its documented depth is 69 feet. Bob Hughes, a longtime summer resident of the lake, told a story of dropping an anchor line over 100 feet and never hitting bottom. He attributed this to natural springs feeding the bottom of the lake. This picture was taken looking toward the south. Lader's Point can be seen jutting out from the right shore.

This 1854 map of the north half of the lake identifies many of the early residents of the lake community and many geographical differences. Notice that the northernmost part of the lake has wider narrows than today. This is because the lake in 1854 had no dam. The lake emptied out into Nine Mile Creek. The road did not follow the shoreline on the eastern shore. The Otisco Lake water level has been raised twice by dam construction since 1854. Today, the lake extends north into the town of Marcellus. In fact, the narrows are located today approximately where the town line is shown on the map. There are several roads shown here that are now abandoned. The road turning easterly off of Main Street in Amber (see reference mark [A] opposite the J. Worthy house) is Cooley Hill Road. Today, you can see it just as you leave Amber northbound; it is overgrown and very steep. As you proceed southbound through Amber, Amber Road still turns east in the center of town. The next road south of Amber, going from Otisco Valley Road to Patterson Road, does not exist any longer (see reference [C]). In fact, the author and others are not sure exactly where the intersection was actually located. It apparently was located just 150–200 yards south of Amber Road. This road was not shown on an 1889 map. Then, the next intersecting road south of Amber was part of the Hamilton & Skaneateles Turnpike (see reference [B]). This portion of the turnpike, which went up Oak Hill, was abandoned in the 1930s. The road turned up Oak Hill in front of Solomon Wheeler's barn, located just a few hundred feet from today's Oak Hill Road. An original 6-foot-tall cement-post road marker remains in front of the barn pointing up the Trendowski driveway and into the woods. The road reappears as a short road or driveway midway up Oak Hill Road, now called Olcott Drive.

Amber is the only village on Otisco Lake. Neighboring villages of Marietta (2 miles to the north), Marcellus (7 miles to the north), Spafford (southwest), Otisco, Navarino, and Borodino have been important to the community's development. Amber and almost half of Otisco Lake are located in the town of Otisco. A small portion of the lake, north of the narrows, is located in the town of Marcellus and the western portion of the lake is in the town of Spafford. This Amber view was taken in 1908.

This is another bird's-eye view of Amber facing west. The establishment in the center is Streeter's Boarding House and its barn. This was one of several boarding houses in Amber and the immediate lake area. Today, this house still exists and is located just north of the intersection of Amber Road and Otisco Valley Road (Main Street in Amber). In the time period of this photograph, early 1900s, Heath's Grove was located on the waterfront to the left of Streeter's, and Lamb's Grove was on the right in the large, dense grove of trees.

This photograph shows a much earlier view of Amber in the winter. The temperature drops below zero degrees many times in a typical winter. Records show the temperature sometimes dropping to 30–40 degrees below zero. With an ice thickness of 12 inches or more, it was common to see horses and wagons, and later, trucks, crossing the lake with heavy loads of hay and other feed. Crossing the frozen lake shortened travel by several miles. Over the years, numerous stories have been told of wagons, animals, and vehicles unexpectedly breaking through the ice. This picture was taken in the early 1900s. Note the row of small cottages on the Amber Beach lakefront. Amber Church is shown on the left.

Looking southeast, this is Lader's Point before the water was raised to its final level in 1908. Notice how much of the land of the point is above water. Today the area is mostly underwater and very shallow. In the mid- to late 1800s, the point was sometimes known as Newville's Point, after the Newville family, who owned land on the point and south.

This view shows the old Pine Lawns area, just north of the cemetery. It was taken from Molzen's hill looking southwest. Davis Grove would be to the right of this photograph.

This view is from the dam looking southward toward the narrows. The main body of Otisco Lake is just beyond the trees. The north end, by the dam, is referred to as the "foot" of the lake and the south end is the "head" of the lake. This naming convention is different from most other lakes.

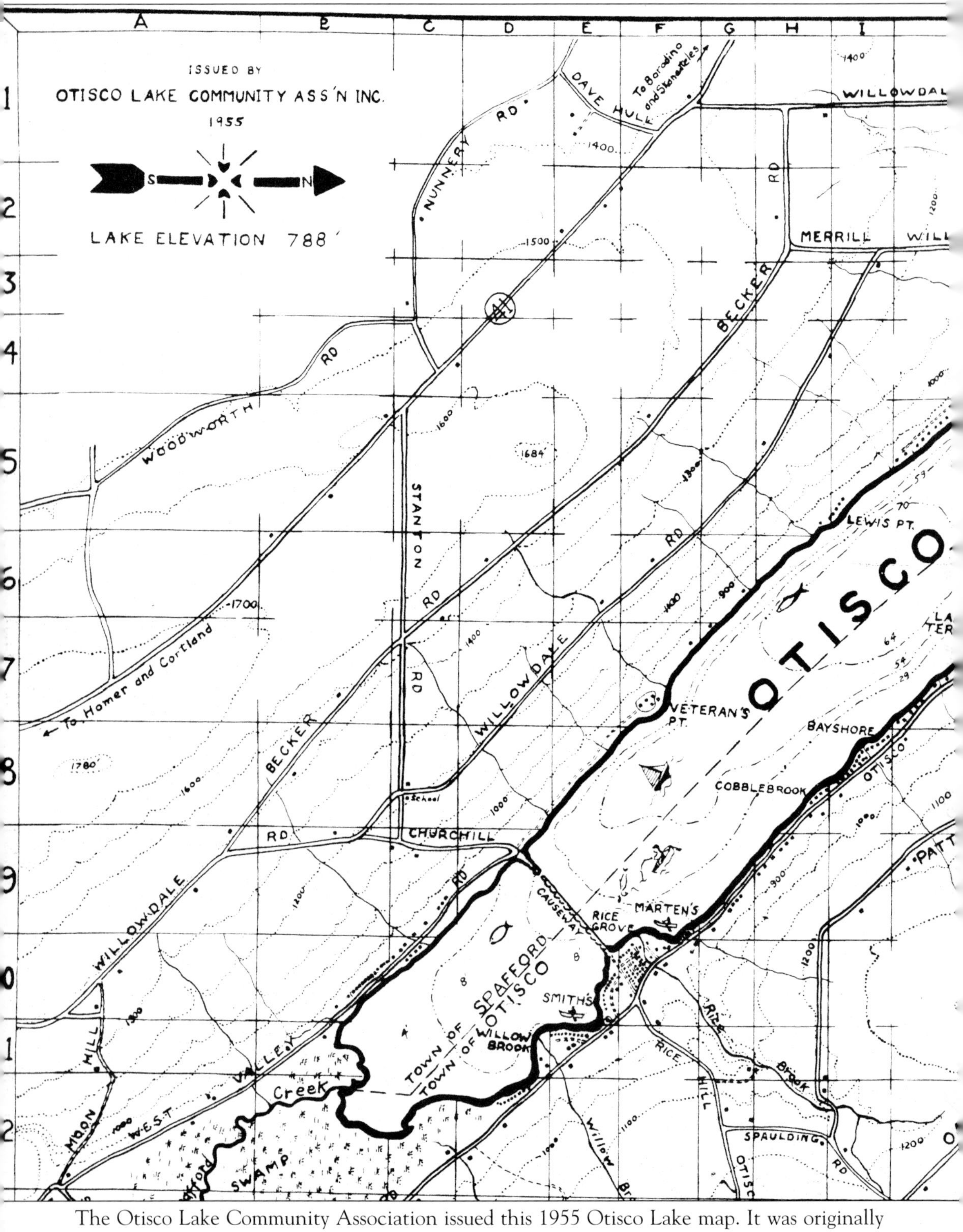

The Otisco Lake Community Association issued this 1955 Otisco Lake map. It was originally

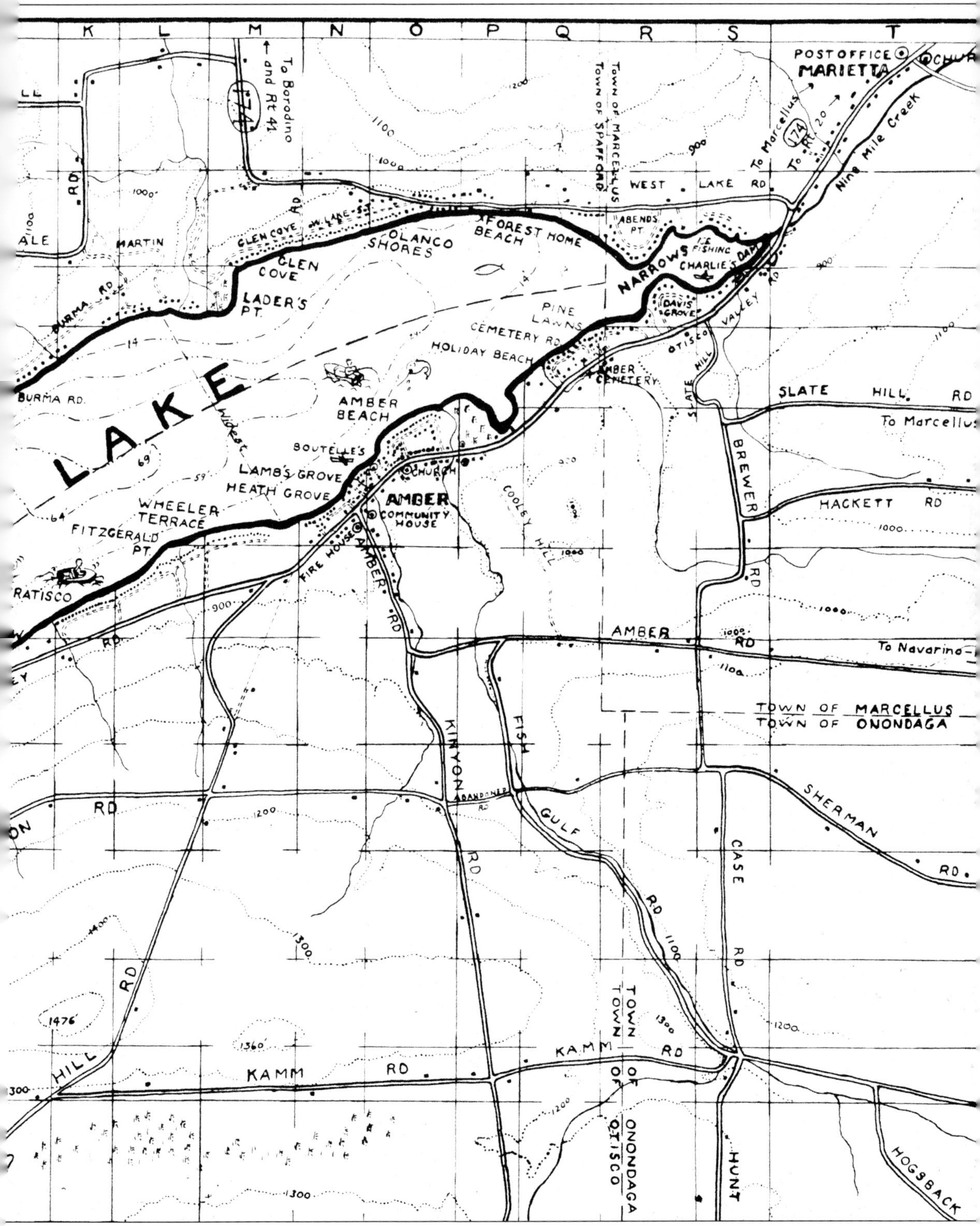

drawn by Phoebe H. MacLeod and was updated in the mid-1970s by Teal Trendowski.

Here is a 1932 postcard greeting from Otisco Lake. The top of the card says, "It takes real fishermen to land these." The postcard used a 2¢ stamp.

This 1910 postcard cartoon states, "I'm not having any luck here at Amber, NY" with the bird eating the fisherman's bait. Otisco Lake was well known as a tourist resort area.

Two

Lake Front Community

Landowners and visitors have always shared a common sense of community because of the lake. Otisco Lake's beauty is unmistakable in any season. This photograph shows Amber Landing in 1911.

This is Fitzgerald Point in 1913. The row of trees follows the access road today. Notice how barren the shoreline is of trees; there were few of them planted across the properties until the 1920s.

Here is the same view as above, but notice the boathouse at the end of the point. It was owned by the King family.

The Fitzgerald homestead was located just above Fitzgerald Point on the lake road. Mr. Fitzgerald sold the surrounding farmland to Solomon Wheeler and in the 1910s–20s sold lake front lots to individuals who subsequently built lakefront cottages. Much of the farmland was sold in 1960 by Ernest Wheeler (Solomon's son) to John Bishop Jr. and Barbara Bishop. A large farm, located south of the Fitzgerald homestead during the early 1900s, was owned by Walter and Belle Bishop, and subsequently owned by John and Grace Bishop. Esther McAvoy and her son Robert lived in this house in the 1930s.

These cottages were on the north side of Fitzgerald Point. The photograph was taken in approximately 1910. The cottages belonged to, from left to right, the Schroeder, Dunlap, and Thompson families.

Camp Ethelia was one of the first cottages built on Fitzgerald's Point. It was built and is still owned and used by descendants of the Dunlop family—Robert Munro, Ann Dolan, and grandchildren. Notice the Model-T car on the right. This photograph was taken *c.* 1921.

Next door to Camp Ethelia was Camp "LAF A LOT." This camp still exists and is owned by Beth Nash.

This photograph shows the Dunlop family at their cottage, called Camp Ethelia, on Fitzgerald Point. The next door neighbors, the Schroeder family, are camping out in a tent. Eventually, their camp was called Camp LAF A LOT.

This photograph, taken around 1910–15, shows the south side of Fitzgerald Point.

This photograph shows an aerial view of Wheeler Terrace in 1948. Wheeler Terrace is the next set of cottages north of Fitzgerald Point. It was named after Solomon Wheeler, who sold the lakefront properties in 1910–20.

This 1920s view shows the east side of Wheeler Terrace. Notice the lack of trees. Today, the trees are 80 feet tall and appear to be in a straight row across Wheeler Terrace and Fitzgerald Point properties; all are about the same maturity. A longtime resident says that a tree salesman passed through the area in 1920 or 1921 and successfully sold a large number of "North Carolina poplar" trees to lake cottage residents.

North of Wheeler Terrace, before you reach Heath's Grove, is a cove. The shoreline and adjoining farmland was owned by Solomon Wheeler and his son Ernest. This photograph is from 1922. The beginning of Heath's Grove is on the left.

Sailing in the cove between Wheeler's Terrace and Heath's Grove was a favorite activity even in 1925.

These bathers are enjoying themselves at Heath's Grove in 1921. Heath's Grove provided popular entertainment to both local residents and visitors. Some of the activities included dancing at Heath's Dance Hall (with round and square dances every Wednesday and Saturday night throughout the summer), a baseball field with a locally sponsored baseball team in the 1920s through the 1940s, picnics, parades, boat and canoe races, and of course, swimming.

This is another view of Heath's Grove in the early 1920s. Heath's Grove hosted major clubs' picnics, as did other entertainment spots around Otisco Lake (Davis Grove, Lamb's Grove, Rice Grove, and Forest Home). Some of the major organized gatherings were as follows: 1) the "Six Town Picnic," where people from neighboring towns of Otisco, Marcellus, Tully, Skaneateles, Spafford (including Borodino), and Onondaga gathered once a year; 2) the Farmer's Picnic; 3) the Civic League picnic; and 4) school picnics.

This postcard photograph taken around 1909–10 shows the Heath's Grove shoreline a year after the lake water level was raised. Prior to this period, the shore was located past the trees. On the back of this postcard is a 1¢ stamp and a message from Eda Witer to Elizabeth Falmestock of Syracuse which reads, "Are you not sorry to miss seeing Amber this year?"

Heath's barn and the Heath's Grove shoreline is shown in this approximately 1910–15 photograph. The stone retaining-wall was built in 1908 for George Heath by William Malley of Marcellus. This 500-foot-long, 8-foot-high wall was made from squared blocks quarried in Marcellus at the old O'Halloran stone quarry.

This postcard, dated 1909, shows Heath's Grove looking north. Heath's barn is located on the left of this picture. After the retaining wall was built, four of six cottages were moved back 10 to 50 feet. The earth level was raised and seeded and Carolina poplar trees were planted. A wide stone stairway was built and a floating dock installed for boats.

The shoreline and cottages are at Heath's Grove in 1907.

This is the shore off Heath's Grove before 1908 when the lake level was raised.

Bathing at Heath's Grove in 1905 was a popular activity. Notice that there are several docks and boats on the shoreline. Swinging on a rope from a tall tree was also great fun.

These children are rowing in front of one of the cottages in Heath's Grove in 1909. Charles Bouttelle and his son Petey were expert craftsmen in building boats similar to this one. Charles also built canoes at his boathouse in Amber.

Pictured here are Heath's Grove cottages in the mid-1920s. The woman with the apron is Ruby Heath. Starting in 1934, the Otisco Lake Civic League (predecessor to the Otisco Lake Community Association) held their annual picnic at Heath's Grove.

This 1920s photograph shows Dr. Ayling's cottage, which was located at the northern end of Heath's Grove. The cottage, even though separated by an access road and stream, was actually part of Lamb's Grove.

Here is another view of Dr. Ayling's cottage from about the same time period, the 1920s. Notice the access road that leads up to Main Street in Amber. This plot of land was purchased in 1901 when it was an apple orchard. The cottage was built in 1902. The sea wall was built along with Heath's wall in 1908.

Amber Landing was also located at the site shown in the previous photograph. Taken in 1909, this photograph shows the *Fontney* arriving at Amber Landing, where passengers would then walk up the access road to Main Street in Amber. As they approached Main Street, they would pass the icehouse and Amber Creamery on the left. Also on the left was Lamb's Grove; on the right was Heath's Grove. Streeter's Boarding House was located almost directly across Main Street.

The *Fontney* carried passengers and delivered mail to several places on the lake. This photograph is of the Amber Landing dock in 1909.

Lamb's Grove was the next group of cottages north of Heath's Grove between Heath's Grove and Bouttelle's boat livery. Similar to other privately owned cottage communities on Otisco Lake (and in almost all resort areas), Mr. Lamb rented these cottages to tourists and repeat summer visitors.

This is the Lamb's Grove shoreline in 1906. The Amber Landing dock is shown in the center of the photograph. Heath's Grove is just beyond the dock.

This is Lamb's Grove in 1907 before the lake water level was raised. These boats were reserved for the guests who stayed in the cottages in the grove. Rowboats were used exclusively since outboard motors were not yet readily available.

Amber Church can be seen in the background in the center of this photograph. This is the Amber shoreline by Lamb's Grove in 1908.

A postcard to Miss Ara Hunt of Skaneateles dated August 20, 1907, says, "I am having a fine time . . . Jessie." The postcard used a 1¢ stamp.

Here is another dock on Lamb's Grove shoreline. Fitzgerald Point can be seen in the distance.

A postcard dated July 22, 1910, shows several Lamb's Grove cottages.

Lamb's Grove is shown from a distance in this 1912 photograph. Bouttelle's inlet is located to the left. Amber Landing and the access road separating Heath's Grove and Lamb's Grove is shown on the right.

This is Bouttelle's Boat Livery sometime between 1908, after the lake water level was raised, and 1914, when a second boathouse was constructed. It was the only boat livery on Otisco Lake in the late 1800s and one of two boathouses in the early 1900s.

This is the Spencer cottage near Bouttelle's Boat Livery. The postcard photograph was dated 1910. The Amber Church is in the distance on the left. To the right would be Bouttelle's Boat Livery.

For many years, local residents and visitors would come to Bouttelle's to swim. The roof of the new boathouse can be seen behind the old boathouse. Spencer's cottage is in the center of this photograph taken in approximately 1915–18.

This is the view in 1915 from Bouttelle's Boat Livery, looking north to Amber Beach cottages. Notice how far out from the beach the cottages seem to be located.

This photograph shows the Hotchkiss house on the left and the Lakeside Inn on the right. The Hotchkiss house is located next to the Amber Grocery Store today. This view is from the lakefront looking east toward Main Street.

On the right is Amber Beach with one cottage showing. Dean and Dorland Smith are enjoying their boat with a friend aboard in 1921.

Here are Amber Beach cottages as they were in 1905–1907. Before the dam raised the water level the second time in 1908, an access road ran in front of the cottages as this photograph shows. Afterward, the road was relocated behind the buildings. Nelson Weeks is the gentleman standing to the right of the cottages.

Here are the same cottages several years later. This photograph postcard is dated 1915.

Kamp Kozy, owned by William Gorham, was located on Amber Cemetery Road. This photograph shows campers in 1901. Mr. Gorham is the man sitting on the dock post in the front cover photograph of this book.

This photograph shows boating on the lake in 1920. This lakefront appears to be the Holiday Beach or Pine Lawn.

This 1880s drawing shows the farm and residence of John Van Benthuysen, located just south of the cemetery. On the 1955 map in this book, the lake cottage area is called Holiday Beach. Notice that the creek meanders from the right to the left and flows into the lake. Today, this creek flows under the Otisco Valley Road in approximately the same place that it did over 100

years ago. The artist's viewpoint for this drawing was looking west to Otisco Lake and Spafford Hills in the distance. To the south (left) is the village of Amber. To the north (right) is the dam and the village of Marietta.

The first stone dam was built in 1868, and in 1869 the lake level was raised to make it a feeder for the Erie Canal. An award was paid to people losing land to the enlarged lake. For example, Sarah A. Eddy received $356 as payment for a little more than four acres. Her property was on the east side of the lake (south of John and Grace Bishop's property, today). Tobacco fields located in the valley were flooded with the raising of the first dam. In addition, a horseracing track in front of Amber Church was flooded. This photograph of the dam was taken in 1903.

This photograph shows the second dam in 1910.

The original lake level was 772 feet above sea level. The 1868–69 dam raised it 9 feet to 781 feet above sea level. In 1908 the lake level was raised again, this time by 4 feet, 9 inches, to 785 feet and 9 inches above sea level. Otisco Lake provided drinking water for neighboring towns of Salina, Clay, Cicero, Manlius, Camillus, and Marcellus. This 1914 photograph shows the remains of an old dam in front of the new structure.

A photograph of the dam from a 1915 postmarked postcard.

This 1908 photograph shows the construction of the second dam. Notice the lake shoreline and the roadway. There was quite a large area of dry land between the shoreline and road because the water level was low while construction took place. Also notice the large mechanical crane to the left of center in this photograph.

This is a close-up of the construction of the dam in the early winter season. The crane is working on the west shoreline in front of the actual dam. Both the crane and the dock are the same as shown in the previous photograph.

This is a view of the lower lake area looking southeast from the dam. The photograph was taken approximately between 1910–15. Remnants of the old dam structure are being used as a dock for fishing.

This is a view of the narrows from the dam looking south.

This photograph shows two cottages located near Burma Road on the west shore of the lake. The second one is partly obscured by the trees. Midway down the west side of the lake is a road and terrain that defies description, Burma Road. The land bordering the lake has steep hillsides, deep ravines, large trees, and beds of shale rock. Prior to the 1930s, there was no road to the lake shore area now occupied by Burma Road properties. The few camps that existed were accessible only by boat or by a long hike down to the valley from Willowdale Road, which made building these camps a great challenge. The shore line was a vertical 250-foot drop from the top of the hill. The first camps to be built (before the road) were owned by the Biehler, Luhr, Nightingale, Weil, Wendell, Nalton, Armstrong, Kemper, and Malcolm families. A 15-foot right-of-way, which led down from Willowdale Road, was acquired in 1930–31 by Mr. Biehler from the Pendergasts'. In 1941, the residents decided to build Burma Road. Mr. Pendergast, the land owner, agreed to extend the road plan further to accommodate more potential cottages. He also helped furnish labor and equipment. The four key people starting the project were Pendergast, Armstrong, Wendell, and Weil in late 1941. Construction continued for more than ten years, extending the road to include new camp lots. Many loads of gravel had to be brought as well as culverts to fill the deep ravines and level the road. In 1952, the Burma Road Association was formed with 28 camp-property owners for the purpose of handling road problems and maintenance. The first chairman was Pete Napier.

This postcard is from the summer of 1911. The postcard says, "My two men went for a 25-mile bicycle trip today going around Otisco Lake, Sincerely, Mrs. C.A. Moule of Skaneateles."

Camping on the west shore was always a rough, frontier-like challenge, since few roads or driveways led to the waterfront.

This is Main Street, on the east side of Amber. Amber had sidewalks in the early 1900s. Jones's Store (the second building from the right) was located next to his residence (the building on the far right).

The Odd Fellows Hall was located across from the James Niles home in the late 1800s and a few hundred yards north of the present Amber Grocery Store. This building was first used as a tobacco shed, where tobacco leaves were stripped from the plant and baled. After that, the structure was used as a meeting lodge, and in the early 1930s it served as an auditorium for plays and as a dance hall. Otisco Lake can be seen in the background to the right of the building.

Streeter's Boarding House was located in the center of Amber on Main Street. This photograph was taken in 1915. In the 1940s, the front portion of the house was removed by owner George Oster and replaced with two rooms. Today, the main house actually consists of the additions to the original structure. It is currently owned by Peter and Nancy Oster.

This is a side view of Streeter's Boarding House in the late 1800s. Notice that there were no window shutters on the house during this period.

This photograph shows Orrin Smith, Net Smith, and their daughter, Violet Smith (Mrs. Louis Stafford), around 1900. The house is located on the left approximately 1/3 mile east on Amber Road from Main Street in Amber.

The Burroughs sisters and their mother (standing), shown outside their home, maintained the first telephone exchange in the area. Their house was located across from and slightly north of the church.

This is Clifford Lamb's house in 1912 located on Main Street in Amber at the entrance to Lamb's Grove. Shown on the left is the Amber Creamery and behind that is the ice house.

In the late 1800s and early 1900s, this was a boarding house located across the road from the southern part of Heath's Grove. It was the residence of Leon Bishop. The house was torn down in the mid-1960s.

Alfred J. and Diana Niles built this Amber house in 1867 and the neighboring store in 1861. Subsequently, the house and adjacent store were owned by Byron Grennell (1890s), then by Miles and Adeline Grinnell (1922). In the mid-1940s, the house was purchased by Roscoe and Minnie Bennett, followed by Jack and Lula (Bennett) Richards. It was torn down around 1970 to make room for the Amber Superette parking lot. Notice the very unusual rounded porch on the front corner. This photograph was taken in the early 1920s when the Grinnell's lived here. It is very unusual for two families with very similar names (but spelled differently) to own the same house and store.

This 1878 drawing shows the Hillyer family home and harness shop, which are located just north of the present-day Amber Store. Myron and son Horton were partners in the "harness making trade" in Amber during the mid-1800s. The harness shop is now gone. The home has had several owners after the Hillyers, including B. Kenyon (purchased 1888), Alison Cowles, Tobias Eibert, and Louis and Estella Oster. It is presently owned by Cy and Pat Vile.

This 1920s photograph shows the farmhouse owned by Solomon Wheeler. Located south of Amber at Otisco Valley Road and Oak Hill Road (current name), this house was purchased by Stanley and Ethel (Wheeler) Trendowski in the mid-1940s. They operated fish bait and vegetable businesses from their house until 1995. Before Oak Hill Road was built, the main road east bound toward Otisco and Tully was the Hamilton & Skaneateles Turnpike. Part of this turnpike ran up Oak Hill, where the Trendowski's driveway is now located. The road was abandoned in the mid-1930s.

Solomon Wheeler's barn was located across from the farmhouse shown at the top of the page. The barn and the house were built in 1871. Above the roof of the main barn was a "cupola," which helped vent hot air out of the barn during summer months.

Overturned in a violent windstorm in December 1921, this rental cottage was located in Heath's Grove.

A historical presentation of the Otisco Lake community would not be complete without honoring the dedicated volunteer fire company that has served area residents since 1949. This photograph was taken approximately in 1956. A few of the firemen in this parade are Ellis Henderson (carrying the flag), Ed Hillenbrand and Walt Travers (carrying the banner), and Fire Chief Ed Bright (wearing the white hat).

The Amber Fire Department's first pump-truck was a 1949, 6-cylinder Ford, capable of pumping up to 500 gallons of water per minute. It carried only 500 gallons and had a 2-speed axle. Shown here on the left is Ed Bright, the first fire chief, and on the right is Cecil Olcott, the president and chaplain. This photograph was taken around 1950.

The Amber Fire Department and the Otisco Lake Community Association hosted parades for the town residents and visitors almost every year. This photograph was taken about 1950–52 in front of Amber Church. Newman's Garage is located in the background. The group of men shown on the left are veterans from the Marietta Veteran's Post. The lead fireman holding the flag is Walt Travers. The two men directly behind him are Ed Hillenbrand (left) and Cecil Olcott. The fireman directly behind them is Wally Snyder.

Children always seem to enjoy parades, especially the firetrucks. The Amber Fire Department still has this truck and uses it for parades in Amber and neighboring towns.

Often the Amber Fire Department volunteered to participate in other town's festivals. Activities included a parade, of course. But most exciting was the "push-ball" contest between the two towns' fire departments. Each group of firemen lined up on opposite ends of an exhibition field. An overhead wire had a large ball hanging on it. Then, each group of firemen, dressed in full fire-fighting gear, sprayed water to force the ball to their opponent's side to win. The cars along this parade route are, from left to right, a 1946 Dodge, a 1940 Ford, a 1948 Chevy, and a 1951 or 1952 Packard.

Three

Commerce and Work

Bouttelle's Boat Livery was one of several important businesses on Otisco Lake. This picture, taken around 1900, shows the original building and Amber Church in the background. Charles Bouttelle built and rented boats and was also a fishing guide. Pictured, from left to right are, Floyd McManus, Mr. Myer (sitting in the boat), John McAvoy, Ernest Bouttelle (known as Petey), Charles Bouttelle (father of Ernest), and Hank Streeter. Charles Bouttelle repaired up to 50 rowboats and canoes each winter. During the summer months, he operated a very successful boat rental business.

Strings of boats hooked together and anchored at each end were a common sight in front of Bouttelle's Boat Livery. The swamp grass near the shore indicates that this picture was taken before the lake level was raised, probably around 1904–1905. Charles Bouttelle started the boat livery business when Otisco Lake was a "fair size pond" before the lake was raised in 1869. After his death in 1940, his son, Ernest (Petey) Bouttelle, continued the boat rental business and also rented small cottages on the property.

A new boathouse was built in 1914 by Harley, Frank, and Leon Bishop, and Petey Bouttelle. This original 1914 structure did not survive, although it resembles the large boathouse on the property today. The new boathouse, shown above, burned in 1918. Some say the fire was caused by firecrackers. This probably explains why Petey was against fireworks being set off near his property on Fourth of July holidays. The camps shown in the background to the right of the boat livery are in Lamb's Grove, a vacation spot for many visitors. Today, the new boathouse, adjoining cottages, and Lamb's Grove are owned by Bill and Marian Settineri.

Olmsted's ice cream stand, located near Lamb's Grove, was the first in Amber. Olmsted's served many kinds of homemade ice cream through the 1950s, including a delicious orange-pineapple flavor.

The Olmsted family also sold their ice cream from a rolling ice-cream parlor. Marjorie and Leonard Olmsted are standing in the doorway. Leonard was better known as "Buster." Their father was Orson Olmsted. Charles Bouttelle is standing outside eating an ice cream cone.

About 40 local and regional farmers brought cream to the Amber Creamery, located between Lamb's Grove and Heath's Grove. Owned by Louis Edinger, the building was originally a blacksmith shop but was rebuilt as a creamery.

Here is another photograph of the creamery. Bricks of butter were made by hand with the aid of a butter printer. The largest production in one day was 2,156 pounds of butter. Wagons would start for Syracuse at 2 a.m. to deliver the butter to 1,600 customers. The building was torn down in 1977. The Amber icehouse can be seen to the left behind the creamery.

During the 1800s and early 1900s, the town's people and businesses relied on ice for refrigerating their milk, butter, and other perishable foods. Large blocks of ice were taken from the lake and stored in the Amber icehouse for use in the summer. Sawdust was shoveled over the ice to preserve it in the warm weather. Customers would buy blocks of ice, cut to the size needed to fit in their icebox. As shown above, the large ice blocks were marked off, cut with saws, and hauled to the storage building. This picture from the early 1900s was taken in front of Heath's Grove and Lamb's Grove.

Blocks of ice taken from the lake are being unloaded and stored in the icehouse next to the creamery. There were four ice houses in the Amber area—one located in back of the creamery, a second across the access road in Heath's Grove (near Olmsted's ice cream parlor), a third one at Lakeside Inn (also called Maxwell's), and a fourth one in Davis Grove. On the left is John Head; on the right is Jim Henderson.

Jones' General Store was located two buildings north of the church in Amber. The 1854 map in this book identifies this building as the Adam's Store. It was torn down in 1940 and an empty lot now exists on the site. Jones' home is located on the right. The church is located further right, out of view in this photograph. During the 1930s, this building was headquarters for the *Clarion* summer newspaper put out by residents of Amber Beach.

This photograph shows the Lakeside Inn in 1908. Over the years, it was also called Amber Hotel, Maxwell's (in the 1930s), Bondy's (1950s), and finally the Amber Inn. In the late 1800s and early 1900s, a large barn belonging to the inn was located along the side of it on Main Street.

Byron C. Grennell's store and post office (all in one building) was located in Amber in the same approximate location as the present-day Amber Store. This mid-1890s photograph identifies several local residents. Pictured are, from left to right, Azariah Hall (uncle to Mr. and Mrs. B.C. Grennell), Orson Olmsted (in the doorway), Heman Griffin, William W. Beers, Captain Moffett, and Wheeler White. Byron Grennell was the postmaster in Amber from 1893 to 1899. Byron Grennell owned both this store and the adjacent house from approximately 1885 to 1904. A few years later, both store and house were owned by Miles and Adeline Grinnell (different family name).

Louis J. Edinger's delivery truck is parked in front of the Amber Store in 1934. Louis and Estella Oster purchased the store in 1924 and W.W. Harper, brother-in-law to Louis Oster, operated it. Estella was postmaster in Amber during most of the 1930s. Louis Oster peddled eggs and butter (made in the Amber creamery) in Syracuse for L.J. Edinger. Beverly (Oster) Schmidt is standing on the truck's running board.

In front of the barn alongside the Lakeside Inn, a horse pulls a farm steam engine. A water pump shown in the foreground was probably used to fill the steam engine's water tank. A revolving belt ran from the engine to power the machine (either a corn husker or threshing machine) on which Pat Dugan is sitting. The barn was torn down in the early 1950s.

The Heath and Kinney General Store and post office (all in one building) was located in central Amber. The building later became the site of Olmsted's ice cream parlor. Today, the building provides apartments.

This early 1900 picture shows a prominent hotel, called Forest Home, located on the west shore of Otisco Lake. It later was named Stadler's Hotel, and then renamed Forest Home again. Today, this is a restaurant called the "Footprint."

Here is an advertisement for the 1907 Farmer's Picnic at Forest Home.

This is Forest Home viewed from the lake in a 1912-postmarked card.

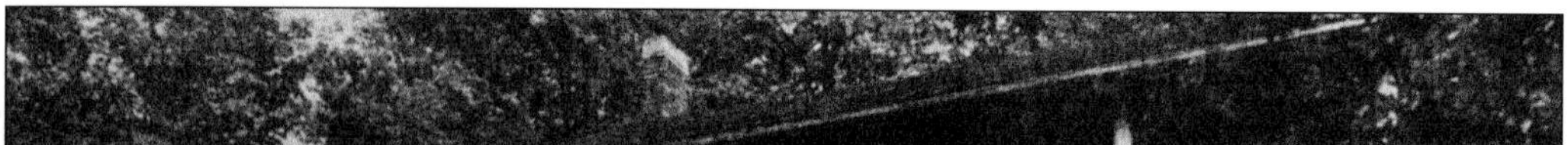

Stadler's Hotel in the late 1930s is shown in this photograph. It was named Forest Home before and after this period.

The Marietta House, an Otisco Lake landmark in the village of Marietta, was a popular stop for tourists wanting food and overnight accommodations. This photograph is from 1914. The building burned to ruins in May 1935. Proprietors of the establishment, Mr. and Mrs. Donald Dillon, were convinced that the fire was started by a "firebug" (arsonist) because it apparently broke out on the outside of the structure.

Here is an invitation to a Christmas party at the Marietta House on December 23, 1892. Music was provided by Flanagan's Full Orchestra. Tickets were priced at a hefty $1.25 per person.

This is King's General Store in Marietta during the 1910s–20s. It became Herman Hunt's Store in 1920, then R.D. Hunt's Store in 1923. Around 1945 it was purchased by Winfield Clarke and today this building houses apartments.

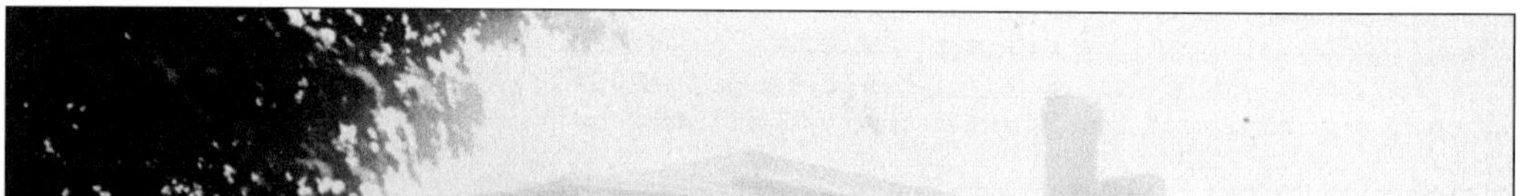

This is the Hunt's Store in the early 1940s with a food sign on the side of the building and an ice cream sign in front. The main gasoline pump is on the right, with an additional pump and a tank on the front porch of the store, probably for fuel oil or kerosene. After Clarke purchased the store in 1945, it became the Marietta Post Office during the mid-1950s.

There have been at least four post offices that have served Marietta and the surrounding communities. One post office in 1891 was located on Sevier Road at the gristmill. Then in the late 1890s, it moved to the Hunt Store. Next, in the 1920s, it moved to a small brick building located across the main road from Sevier Road (shown above in this late 1930s photograph). This office had national recognition as the smallest post office in America. In 1959, the post office was moved back to the old Hunt Store, now owned by Clarke. In 1985, the post office was relocated to its current site about a half-mile toward Otisco Lake.

Marietta Mills was located across Nine Mile Creek on Sevier Road, which adjoins the Marietta church. It was a gristmill that processed wheat and other grains into flour. A large, millstone could be seen near the road many years after the mill was torn down in the 1940s. A large pond located beside the mill was fed by Nine Mile Creek from Otisco Lake. The water powered the mill's equipment to process the grain. The millpond was drained at the same time the building was torn down.

Ed Bailer leads oxen pulling a drag to break up soil for planting in the early 1900s. The field is located south of Amber near the intersection of what is now called Oak Hill Road and Otisco Valley Road.

Solomon Wheeler's oxen are pulling a wagon full of hay. This picture was taken at his barn just south of Amber (the barn can also be seen in the photograph at the top of the page). During the early 1900s, some of the grain grown in the area was taken to Marietta Mills for processing or to the Marietta train station for shipment to other towns. The train loading dock was located approximately where the Marietta Post Office is today.

Early in the 1900s, farmers began to use mechanized equipment such as steam-powered tractors and threshing machines. A threshing machine was used to separate wheat or oats from the straw. This tractor was owned by Edgar Gambell (seated on the tractor). Also pictured are Del Fellows (standing) and Pat Dugan (behind the horses). The tractor was operated by steam and put out a whopping 25-horsepower.

This photograph shows Beebe's portable sawmill in 1909. Charles Olmstead is driving the oxen. Frank Beebe and another unidentified man are located in the background. This photograph was taken in front of Bert Webster's barn near the road that went from Amber to Marietta.

The Murphy farm was located south on Otisco Valley Road near Sawmill Road. Murphy's used this steam engine to power corn-husking equipment. Pictured are Henry Murphy, Grant French, Jim Murphy, W. Belle, L. Masters, Patsy Norris, and Pat, Kate, and Jim Murphy.

Walter Bishop (beside the wagon) and Jim Bonell (on top) have just loaded the wagon with oats. This was taken at the Bishop farm on the east side of Otisco Lake.

Dear Neighbor—

We depend upon you and other motorists in this community for our livelihood.

Naturally, we can't afford to give you bad service and risk losing patronage.

We know gasoline — that's our business — and that's why we urge you to try a tankful of Blue Sunoco, the motor fuel which gives high-test performance, high knockless power and long mileage — at regular gas price.

We're looking forward to seeing you — regularly.

NEWMAN'S SUNOCO SERVICE STATION
Road Service
AMBER, N. Y.

In 1936, the Sunoco gasoline station was flourishing. Owned by Jim Newman, the gas station was one of two in the lake community. (The other gas pump was at W. Harper's Store-Amber Store). Fred Morse is pictured at the pump. The station was located approximately where the Amber firehouse is located now. Later, Newman relocated his business across from Amber Church. This advertisement is a folding card. The oval mark is a hole in the card that allows the photograph of Fred Morse and the gas pump to show when the card is folded. In the late 1950s, the building's roof was moved up the hill behind the firehouse and used as the "beer tent" during the firemen's field days celebrations.

In July of 1938, commercial fishermen were brought to Otisco Lake by the state conservation department to catch carp. Carp are predatory fish that eat many species of the lake's game fish. Mr. Wiedner and his six workers caught 9,000 pounds of carp in one week. For a fee of $1,000, they trapped the carp by net and then put them into a 25-by-50-foot "wood holding crib." The fish were then loaded into tankers and transported to market. Most of the carp weighed between 10 and 30 pounds. A half-ton of cracked corn was used as bait. Sheriff Edwin R. Auer holds a 25-pounder in this picture.

Several 30-pound turtles were netted by Edward Bright and Jacob Larsen, commercial fishermen, while clearing Otisco Lake of carp.

Four

Transportation and Roads

Travel around Otisco Lake up through the early 1900s was predominately by horse and wagon. As in most rural areas in the early 1900s, there was increased mechanization and use of trucks, automobiles, and tractors. This resulted in the need to improve local roads as farmers and other businessmen looked for better transportation for goods and services. This is Fred Comstock, the Amber blacksmith, and his dog in a 1914 Model-T Ford.

Early visitors to Otisco Lake commonly used stagecoach and traveled from Marcellus Junction through Marietta to Otisco Lake and Amber, where numerous boarding houses and hotels were located. This is a late 1800s picture of the stagecoach in front of Lakeside Inn in Amber.

By 1906, a combined railway and boat company offered transportation from Marcellus Junction to several points on the lake, delivering mail and passengers. The train also hauled farm goods and grain from the lake region to market. This photograph shows the train entering Marietta station. A passenger car is on the rear and two freight cars are the second and third cars. The coal car is directly behind the engine.

The Marcellus and Otisco Lake Railway Company had its roots in 1897 when a promotion firm from Chicago interested many leading citizens from Marcellus and the surrounding area in the proposition to construct an electric railroad from Martisco to Marcellus (refer to the map on the following pages). The Marcellus Electric Rail Road Company was incorporated on June 4, 1897, with President Mr. Edward Moir and Secretary Mr. Edmund Reed. It was capitalized for $60,000 and construction began in 1898. With less than 2 miles of roadway constructed, the company went bankrupt because of unplanned expenses in removing difficult rock formations. With new funding and new equipment, the construction resumed in 1901 and the Martisco-Marcellus rail construction was completed in late 1901 or early 1902. On June 2, 1905, the financial setup of the line was completed with the Merchants National Bank of Philadelphia, taking $200,000 worth of common stock sold at par. It was named the Marcellus and Otisco Lake Railway Company (M & OL). In 1904, just prior to the new capitalization, a new engine (known as engine No. 1) weighing 65 tons was purchased from Baldwin Locomotive Works. Construction proceeded rapidly and reached the foot of Otisco Lake in 1906. Two passenger coaches were purchased and passenger service started that year. In 1908, Mr. John Steward became general manager of M & OL. The company purchased a Brooks engine that year (known as Engine No. 2). Unfortunately, this train engine, which weighed only 45 tons, proved too light for the job and was difficult to maintain on the rails. Therefore, M & OL purchased the No. 3 engine, weighing 65 tons. It was delivered early in 1912. No. 3 proved to be well adapted for the work and ran on portions of the railway until 1942, when it was sold for scrap. M & OL continued its operation to Otisco Lake through the late 1930s mostly carrying freight and not passengers. By 1940, the freight business between Marcellus and Otisco Lake had declined so sharply that the railroad filed notice for permission to abandon the route. About 1941, the iron train tracks were torn up and salvaged for the war effort.

Once passengers arrived at Otisco Lake via the M & OL rail line, they were met by passenger boats and powerboats of the Otisco Lake Navigation Company. A passenger boat called the *Fontney* was constructed by Louis Henley in 1906 in Phoenix, New York. It was launched in May 1907, following completion of the railroad from Martisco to Otisco Lake. The *Fontney* was 65 feet long, had a 10-foot beam, full cabin, a 3-cylinder 450-rpm gas engine (made by Barber Company), a searchlight, and three watertight bulkheads. The man located at the stern of the boat is Hank Welch.

The *Fontney* was also used for excursions around the lake. It could carry 130 passengers to the various hotels and boarding houses on the lake and it also delivered mail. By 1907, the business for M & OL and the Otisco Lake Navigation Company was excellent. On August 29, the Annual Six Town Farmer's Picnic was held at Forest Home. Some dissatisfaction with the location of the picnic appeared, with the result that the Rose Hill group held their picnic at Davis Grove and Amber put on a picnic at Lakeside Inn. In all about 7,000 people were around Otisco Lake that day and it was a big day for the railroad and the navigation company. The railroad maintained hourly service but had difficulty handling the crowds while the *Fontney* busily transported the picnickers from one picnic to the other and to the railroad station at the dam.

This is Amber Landing and the *Fontney* in 1911. Wheeler Terrace and Fitzgerald Point can be seen in the distance on the left.

The captains were John Nightingale and Harold Nightingale. One of the helmsmen was George Morgan. The *Fontney* was put in dry dock near the dam after the close of the 1913 summer season. It was not used again.

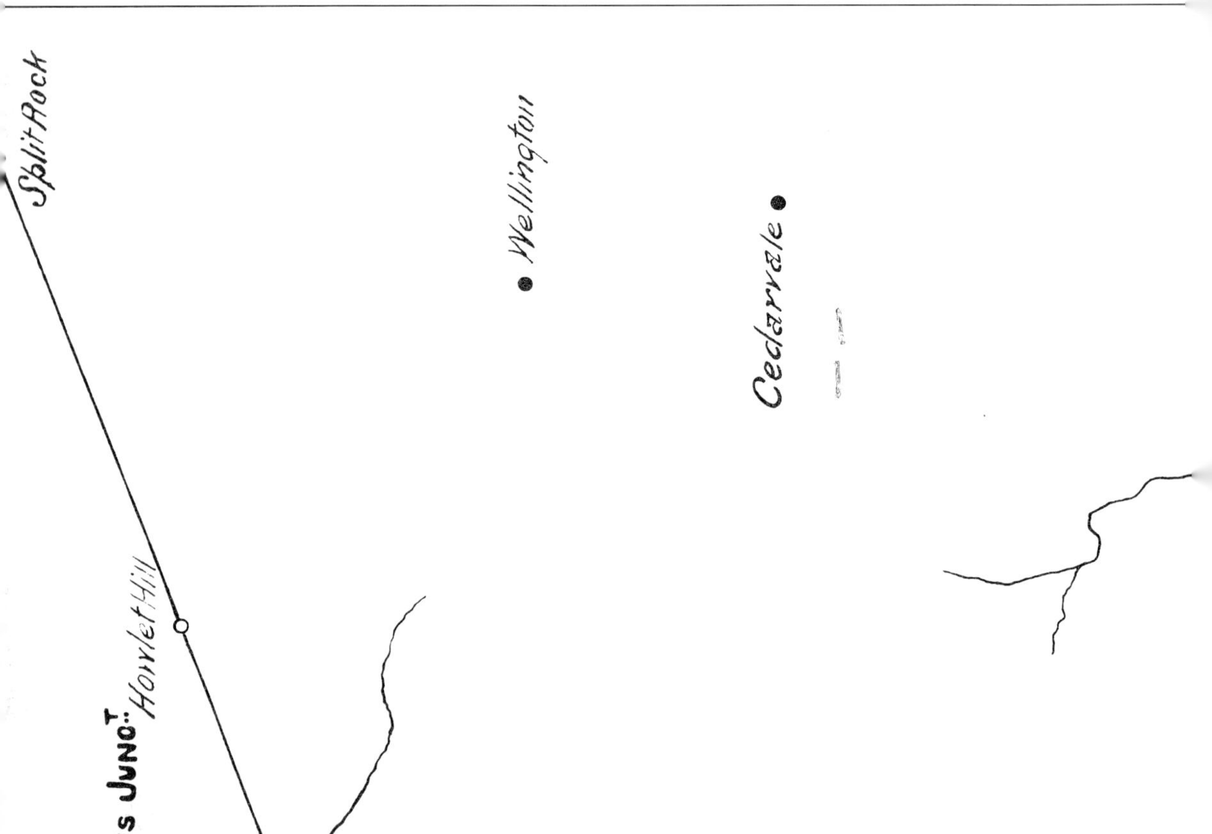

The M & OL rail line route ran from Martisco (Marcellus Junction), through Marcellus, to Otisco Lake. Marcellus Junction provided passengers a convenient station for changing trains bound for Syracuse and Auburn.

The normal route around the lake for the *Fontney* included the dam, Davis Grove, Forest Home, Amber, Royal Glen, Hackett House, Spafford Landing, and Williams House. The Williams Boarding House also went by the name Twin Oaks and was located near today's

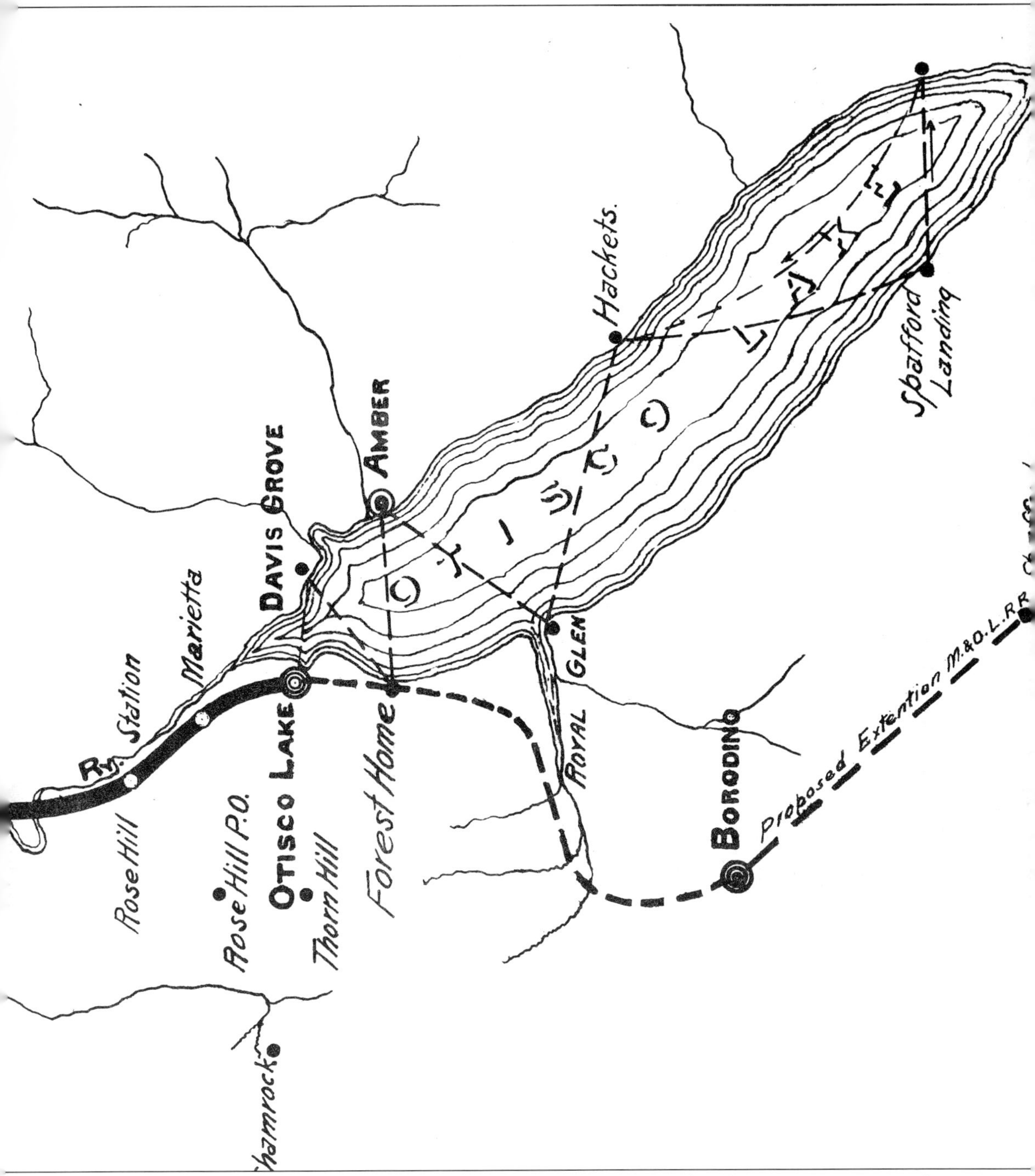

Otisco Lake Marina. The Hackett House was also a hotel or boarding house. At one time the Hackett House owner, Mr. John Hackett and Mr. Bela Patterson, a farmer, decided to switch occupations and properties. After a year, Mr. Hackett was tired of being a farmer and Mr. Patterson was happy to give up hotel ownership. Each returned to his original occupation. Spafford Landing was located at the causeway on the western side of the lake. There was a boarding house located near the landing at the bottom of Church Hill Road.

Marcellus and Otisco Lake Railway Company.

Otisco Lake Navigation Company.

HO! FOR OTISCO LAKE!!!

Season Opens Saturday, May 29th, 1909.

Reached by the Auburn & Syracuse Electric Trolley from Syracuse or Auburn to Marcellus, and via the Marcellus & Otisco Lake Railway to Otisco Lake Station, and to any point on the Lake via the Otisco Lake Navigation Company's boat, "FONTNEY."

The scenery is magnificent; the Air invigorating and the Fishing is GOOD. One day or more on or around the Lake will act as a Tonic to be remembered, and repeated doses will add years to your life.

COME EARLY AND AVOID THE RUSH

TRAINS FROM MARCELLUS TO OTISCO LAKE:

Week days, 7:15 a. m., 10:00 a. m., 4:15 p. m., 6:29 p. m.

Saturdays, 7:15 a. m., 10:00 a. m., 2:30 p. m., 4:15 p. m., 6:29 p. m.

Sundays, 8:00 a. m., 10:00 a. m., 2:00 p. m., 4:00 p. m., 6:30 p. m.

TRAINS FROM OTISCO LAKE TO MARCELLUS:

Week days, 7:40 a. m., 10:25 a. m., 4:31 p. m., 6:54 p. m.

Saturdays, 7:40 a. m., 10:25 a. m., 3:00 p. m., 4:31 p. m., 6:54 p. m.

Sundays, 8:35 a. m., 10:35 a. m., 2:35 p. m., 4:35 p. m., 7:05 p. m.

Correspondence solicited.

JOHN STEWART,

Traffic Manager & Superintendent, Marcellus, N. Y., May 23, 1909.

This is an advertisement for the Marcellus and Otisco Lake Railway Company and the Otisco Lake Navigation Company, dated 1909.

This photograph from around 1910 is facing north at the intersection of Main Street in Amber (now Otisco Valley Road) and Amber Road. Amber Road turns to the right. The building on the right is Streeter's Boarding House. The entrance to Heath's Grove is shown on the left.

Just north of the Amber Church driveway, one can see the sidewalks along Main Street. These sidewalks were lost when the road was widened.

Two horses are pulling a wagon on Main Street in Marietta headed toward Otisco Lake, which is only a few miles away. This photograph, from the early 1900s, is looking north toward Marcellus. Marietta church's steeple and roof can be seen near the center of the photograph.

Here is Main Street in Marietta, again looking north. This stretch of road is closer to the lake than in the previous picture. Notice the well-worn dirt sidewalk on the right.

This photograph shows the dam and adjoining Otisco Valley Road at the north end of the lake. Visitors to the lake still use this fishing spot along the roadway. This 1910 picture was taken after the second dam was built and when automobiles started to use the road more frequently.

This is the same section of road ten years later. An automobile repair garage originally operated by Ed Gosper, then later by Emerson Miner, is on the left of the road just past the dam. The roof of the garage can be seen in the 1910 photograph at the top of the page.

This 1928 photograph shows the hot dog stand and garage, located by the dam and owned at this time by Emerson Miner. The food stand was run by Louis Stafford and his wife, Violet. Fred Smith later turned the tiny eatery into a barbershop, where he cut hair in a 10-by-13-foot room in the front and lived in a room of the same size in the back. The bridge seen on the left crosses Nine Mile Creek just in front of the dam. Next to the garage is a 1926–28 Durant automobile.

This photograph taken in approximately 1905–1907 shows West Lake Road as viewed near Forest Home looking north toward the dam.

This is West Lake Road looking south. Part of Forest Home can be seen on the right. Judging from the improved road and guardrails, this photograph is probably from the early 1920s.

This is a segment along the lake road. The truck appears to be 1915–20 vintage. Does anyone recognize where this segment of road might be located?

Here is a 1930 scene taken from Oak Hill Road. Built in the mid- to late 1920s, this new section of road replaced a three-quarter-mile section of road, which turned up a hill at the Solomon Wheeler house and barn and proceeded up the entire length of Oak Hill. This improved roadway replaced a section of the Hamilton & Skaneateles Turnpike. Today, although the view is just as beautiful, it is obscured by brush and small trees along the road. The village of Amber is just visible on the right of this picture.

This photograph shows the construction of Oak Hill Road just below Ernest Wheeler's farm (halfway up Oak Hill) during the late 1920s. The roof and chimney of Wheeler's house can be seen above the dump truck.

This picture was taken at the corner of Oak Hill Road and the road segment it was replacing (now known as Olcott Drive). The machine was used to make concrete for the roadbed. Ernest Wheeler's house is located out of this photograph to the right. Oak Hill Road had only one lane of concrete (with the other made of gravel) for more than a year while the project was completed.

This is a mid-1920s view of the new route under construction, approximately one-quarter mile after starting up Oak Hill from the lake road.

Construction of Oak Hill Road required the use of a large steam shovel to move great quantities of dirt.

This is the east shore of the lake, just north of the current marina. Even back in the 1910s, cottages were built over the water for the scenic view and efficient use of the lakefront property.

Twin Oaks boarding house can be seen on the east side of the lake road. Matty VanDenbergh of Preble built the Twin Oaks Hotel just before 1900. VanDenbergh sold the hotel to Sam Williams. Francis Tinkham and Jessie Griffin bought it in 1915 and operated the tavern until prohibition. The building was originally located on the lake side of the road but was relocated to the east side of the road in 1916. It was a much smaller cottage-size house when it was on the lakefront. After it was moved, the building was expanded to a large boarding house. Oscar Marten bought Twin Oaks in 1925 and operated it as a "speakeasy" until the end of prohibition (about 1933). Half of the building was torn down in 1927. Bill and Ted Marten, sons of Oscar, built the marina building in 1947 as seen in the photograph above. Bill operated the marina until 1960 when it was sold to Walt Simmons.

At the south end of the lake is a well-known landmark called the causeway. This 1950 photograph shows the abandoned road with overgrown trees much as it is today. However, today the causeway provides a public access area for fishing.

In the early 1900s, the causeway was an important land bridge between the east and west sides of the lake. Before the causeway, this route was used by local Native Americans and English settlers to travel east to west across the valley. In 1868, the State of New York built a stonework dam that increased the water level of Otisco Lake by 9 feet. The dam enlarged the lake by 3 miles in length. A road across the south end of the lake valley connected Churchill Road on the Spafford side with Rice Hill Road on the Otisco side. The lake expansion flooded the road. When the state paid damages to landowners for the flooded land, they promised to rebuild the flooded road. For nearly 28 years, nothing was done. Then an assemblyman brought the matter to the notice of the state legislature and $28,000 was appropriated.

The first causeway, made of hemlock logs, rocks, and gravel, was built to replace the old road. The causeway had one bridge and the state was responsible for causeway repairs. In 1900, the causeway was finished and open for traffic. In 1908, the Suburban Water Company raised the lake 4 feet more. Consequently, the causeway had to be built higher. Toby Eibert blasted out the stone for its foundation. The road was finished for a second time in 1911.

The boarding house shown on the right and sawmill on the left were located on the Spafford side of the causeway. Churchill Road is straight ahead. Workers who labored to build the causeway stayed at the boarding house. This photograph was taken between 1910 and 1915.

This is the causeway as photographed in 1917. There has always been a rumor about a body buried in the causeway. In about 1918, as the story goes, two brothers and a friend were playing cards. When the friend "trumped an ace," one of the brothers became angry and attacked his friend. In self-defense, the man took a stove poker and struck and killed one of the brothers. The two men carried the corpse by horse and wagon down the lake road to the causeway. They supposedly buried the body about halfway across.

This is a rare view of the original bridge that crossed the only opening in the causeway. In 1929, high waters and winds washed the road out so badly that it was impassable. It was not rebuilt. Today, this opening is often used by boats traveling between the south section of the lake and the main lake. Much of the silt, which is washed from streams into the south end of the lake, stays there and is prevented from polluting the main lake water because of this one small opening.

Five

People

People dressed more formally in the late 1800s and early 1900s for "recreational" events than they do today. This photograph shows a typical lakeshore picnic in the 1890s. Notice the men's jackets and bow ties and the women's dresses. Also note the wicker baby carriage in the foreground. This photograph was taken at Camp Kozy located on Amber Cemetery Road. The third person from the left is Louisa French Kasson.

Dorothy Olive Brooks owned property on the east side of Otisco Lake, south of the Bishop's farm. This photograph was taken in 1916.

This photograph shows Adeline (Newman) Burroughs (left) and Nell Newman in the 1880s. Adeline was the mother of Lucy and Stella Burroughs.

This photograph was taken on Armistice Day in 1918. Pictured, from left to right, are Sarah Hill, Dixie Briggs, Mrs. Cantwell, and Mr. Cantwell. Mr. Cantwell was an artist. This photograph was taken near Jones's store, shown in the center of the picture, in Amber.

Charles Bouttelle (front) and others pose near his boathouse in Amber in 1918. His full name was "John Charles Fremont Bouttelle."

Pictured here is Lovilla Colton swimming at Heath's Grove in 1918. Her swimsuit is a very traditional style for the era.

Dr. Charles Baker of Marietta was one of the few doctors serving the Marietta and Otisco Lake area for many years. He is sitting in his new Saxton car in 1915–20.

Pictured here are Margaret and Althea Bishop in 1917. These two girls, their sisters (Pauline and Izelda), and their brother (John) were the children of Walter and Belle Bishop. Otisco Lake can be seen in the background.

Pictured here, from left to right, are Alfred, Althea, Dick, and Margaret Bishop, and Merlyn McBurney in the mid-1920s. Merlyn's mother was Pauline (Bishop) McBurney.

Pictured here, from left to right, are as follows: (front row) Charles Streeter, Sarah Olmsted (aunt to Orson Olmsted), and Henry Streeter (Hank); (back row) the Merrill sisters and Mrs. Streeter. The photograph was taken in front of Mr. and Mrs. Streeter's boarding house on Main Street. Amber Church's parsonage can be seen in the background.

Frank Morgan is riding his horse in Amber after a great snowstorm in the mid-1930s. Maxwell's (Lakeside Inn) is shown on the right and the inn's barn can be seen in the center of the photograph. Frank was well known for training and taking care of horses.

This is Lucy Burroughs in 1931. She and her sister Stella were the operators of the first telephone exchange in Amber. Her switchboard is directly in front with push and pull cords for interconnecting callers. They lived in a house across and slightly north of the church. The Burroughs' sisters took turns sleeping on the living room sofa so they wouldn't miss any late-night calls.

Pictured here are the Ladies of Amber, 1901. From left to right they are as follows: (front row) Birdiene (Beyers) Grennell, Martha Lydel, Ella (Grennell) Olmstead, Maud (Lamb) Weeks, and Lana (Vinton) Bishop; (middle row) Bessie (Harmon) Lamb, Stella Burroughs, Mabel (Weeks) Wheeler, Grace (Bishop) Hickman, and Olivia Abbey; (back row) Celia (Van Benthuysen) Britton, Nina (Williams) Weeks, Mary (Russell) Bishop, Mable (Searle) Morgan, and Lucy Burroughs.

These are the Men of Amber pictured in the 1890s. Notice the string of fish held by those in front.

Pictured here are Stanley and Edith Olmstead, 1910–12. Their mother was Ella (Grennell) Olmstead and their father was Fred Olmstead. This family was not related to the other family living in Amber with a similar name, Olmsted.

This is the Larkin Club of Amber in *c.* 1915. They grouped together to sell Larkin household products door-to-door, such as spices, kitchen instruments, and cleaners. As they sold products, they earned premiums or award coupons, which they could redeem for merchandise. There are three known Larkin desks in Amber today that were purchased with these award coupons. Pictured, from left to right, are as follows: (front row) Bertha Patterson; (middle row) Maud Weeks and Catherine Mahar; (back row) Ina Brown, Sara Lader Lamb, Mrs. Ford, Mabel Wheeler, Louise Head, and Lena Head.

This photograph was taken in front of Bouchey's cottage, near Forest Home, in 1908. Pictured, from left to right, are George Scharoun, Mrs. Felicia Scharoun, Leo Scharoun, Mrs. Clarence Yahn, Misses Matilda, and Marie Scharoun.

Bob Hughes is shown as a teenager at his family cottage on Fitzgerald Point in 1922. A longtime resident, Mr. Hughes traveled every year from Bloomfield, New Jersey, to live the summer season at his cottage on the point. This house is the second from the last at the north end of Fitzgerald Point. The sea wall was built by Bob's father from rocks and boulders lying on the property among the jungle of thorny bushes. The Roark cottage, built in 1920 and now owned by Warren Nolan, can be partially seen on the far right.

This was a theater play at Odd Fellows Hall in 1916. Notice the sign above and center of the room. It states (with artistic license) "Old Mades Convenshun." The cast of characters (not in order) included Adelia Tucker, Mary Bishop, Dixie Briggs, Mrs. Diehl, Ethel Fellows, Nelly Rice, Leora Hotchkiss, Mrs. Comstock, Sarah Hill, Lena Burlton, Mrs. Nightingale, Elsa Rice, Mrs. Gambell, D. Baker, Grace Weeks, Jessie Fellows, Clora Gambell, Josie Lane, Charles Hotchkiss, and Ed Diehl.

Charles and Arabella Bouttelle and their children, Helen and Ernest (Petey), pose at their house in Amber in the late 1800s. Arabella was Nelson Weeks's sister; both came to the United States from England. This house still stands on Main Street of Amber, as does Bouttelle's boathouse, which is located directly behind it.

J. Mashier is riding in his summer stagecoach in approximately 1888. The stage carried passengers and mail between Otisco Lake and Martisco (north of Marcellus).

This portrait shows Gerhardt Kronen (child) and Hubert Kronen I. The portrait was taken approximately in 1893. Hubert came to Otisco Lake in 1903 by horse and buggy from Marcellus. He liked the area so much that he bought the land where his family still lives. This is referred to as the Kronen compound and is located on the lakefront, north of the cemetery. His wife was Anna and his children were Anna, Gerhardt, Marie, and Hubert II.

This is Anna Kronen, approximately 1915–1920, tilling the soil for a garden. Anna was the wife of Hubert Kronen I. Rae Fuller's camp is in the background.

This photograph shows the Kronen's starting to dig a basement for their house in 1923. Pictured, from left to right, are Hubert Kronen I, Gerhardt Kronen, Leonard O'Brien (husband of Anna Kronen O'Brien), and a neighboring farmer.

Shown here, from left to right, are Hubert Kronen II, Jackie (Eastman) Andrews (child), Marie (Kronen) Eastman, Louise Kronen (wife of Gerhardt), Vernice (Kronen) Pikarsky (daughter of Gerhardt), Louise Kronen (wife of Hubert II), and an unidentified other.

This photograph shows Solomon E. Wheeler, who was born in 1842 and died in 1923. He built the house and barn located at the intersection of what is known today as Otisco Valley Road and Oak Hill Road. Solomon owned several farms and land located south of Amber and on Oak Hill, Kinyon Road, and Amber Road.

Ida (Wheaton) Wheeler, Solomon's wife, poses for a photograph. They had one son, S. Ernest Wheeler. The image was taken facing toward the lake in front of their home at what is now known as Otisco Valley Road and Oak Hill Road. One of the barn buildings shown on the right was torn down in the 1960s but the two adjacent main barns remain standing.

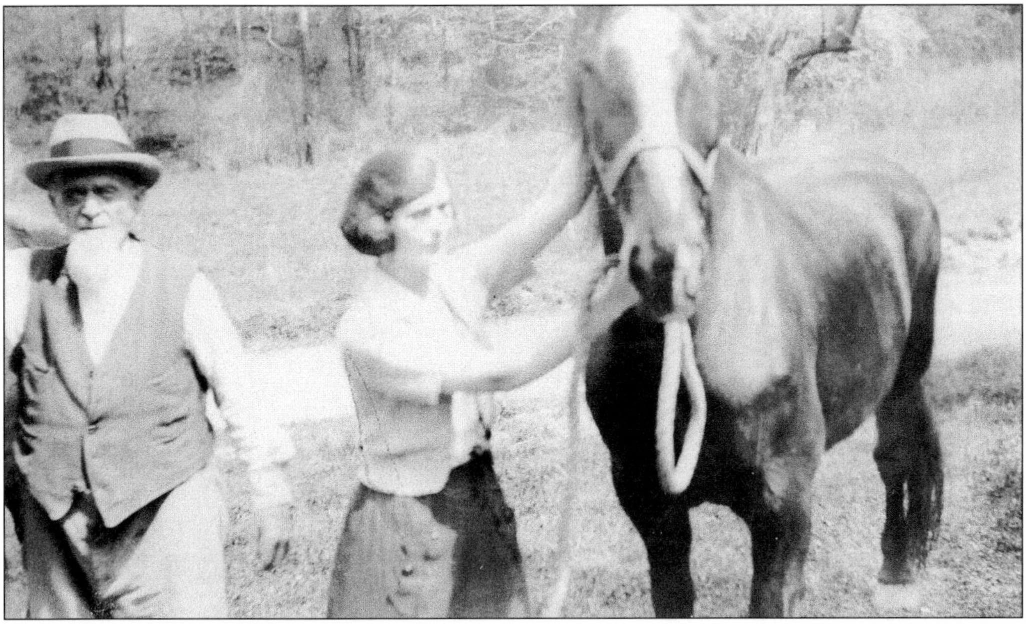

Solomon Wheeler and Izelda Bishop pose for a photographer in approximately 1920. Izelda was the daughter of Walter and Belle Bishop, who owned the next farm south on the lake road.

Ernest Wheeler is hauling wood with his oxen behind his father's barn located just south of Amber. Ernest was born in 1885 and died in 1964. Amber is located less than one-quarter mile to the left. Ernest and wife, Mabel (Weeks) Wheeler, had six children (Marjorie, Clifford, Ethel, Raymond, Edna, and Malcolm), all who have lakefront properties on this original farm located at the foot of Oak Hill Road.

In 1922, a tremendous snowstorm hit the Otisco Lake area. A trench was dug through the snow to the watering troth so that the farm animals could drink. This is Clifford Wheeler, 11 years old, son of Ernest Wheeler, at their farm located on Oak Hill. Otisco Lake valley can be seen in the distance.

Clifford, Ethel, and Marjorie Wheeler are having fun on a bobsled in the mid-1920s.

Clifford Wheeler and a neighbor in front of a farmhouse, located across from Ernest Wheeler's barn on Oak Hill Road in the 1920s. Notice the "long johns" hanging on the clothesline. Without the modern convenience of electric dryers, clothes had to dry outdoors on the line when the weather was good. In the winter, clothes were hung to dry in the basement or the attic.

Catherine Mahar and Raymond Wheeler sitting on the hull of the *Fontney*, c. 1926. Catherine Mahar was a schoolteacher in the Amber area and Raymond was one of her students. Raymond Wheeler operated Wheeler Acres farm and has been the justice of the peace for the town since January 1976.

Clifford Wheeler and Lyndon Bishop in 1923 are playing with their Climax wagon.

Photographed in the mid-1930s, these three women are Wheeler sisters, daughters of Ernest and Mabel Wheeler. Edna Bailer (left), Ethel Trendowski (center), and Marjorie Seeley are all dressed up for Easter services at the church.

Pictured here are the Ladies of Amber. From left to right they are as follows: (front row) Hattie Kenney, Cora Jones, Flora Hotchkiss, Lib Streeter, Ruby Heath, Esther McAvoy, Kitty Lamb, Willard Lamb (boy), and Sara Hill; (back row) Ada Bishop, Ida Wheeler, Kittie Lamb, Ellen Kinney, Emma Heath, Lena Heath (child), unidentified, Mrs. Clinton Mills, Nora Streeter, Mary Grennell, baby Grennell, Maggie Bishop, Adeline Burroughs, Belle Bishop, and John Bishop (baby). This photograph was taken around 1903. The gentleman in the center is Rev. Lydell.

Clarence Yahn was the longtime owner of Forest Home Hotel. He drowned while fishing across from the hotel after becoming entangled in his fishing line, October 14, 1909.

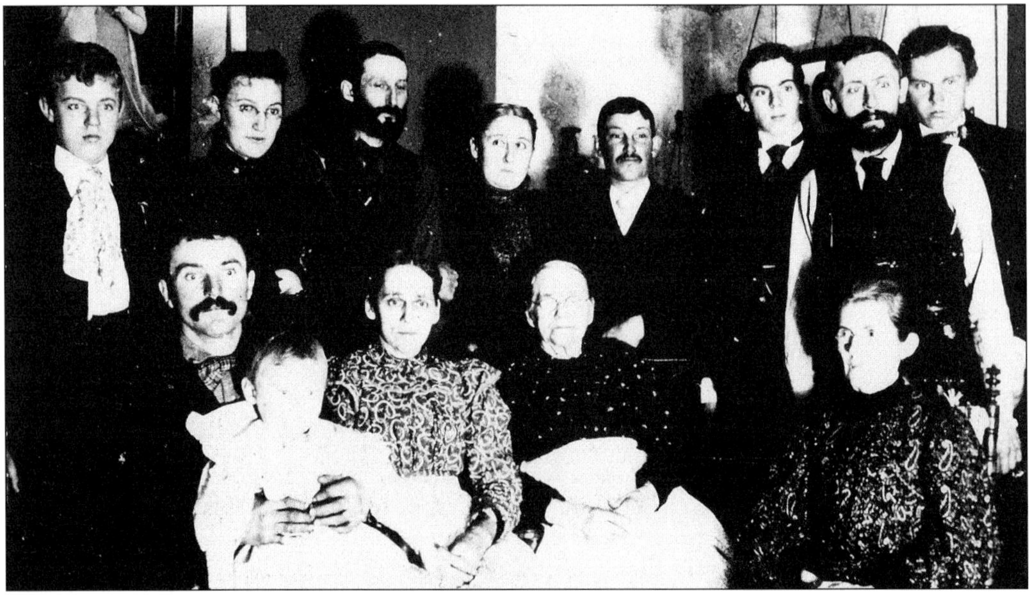

Sitting together in a joint family portrait are the Patterson, Kinyon, and Heath families in 1897. From left to right they are as follows: (front row) Arlow Patterson, Carl Patterson (baby), Flora Patterson, unidentified, and Adelaide Kinyon; (back row) Munson Kinyon, Bertha Patterson, Charley Patterson, Delphine Heath, Franklin Heath, Charley Kinyon, Byron Kinyon, and Emmet Kinyon.

The Marten family is enjoying boating and swimming in front of the Twin Oaks Hotel in 1923. From left to right are Helen and Ethel (daughters of Henry Marten), Henry Marten (brother to Oscar Marten), Fredricka (daughter of Oscar), Oscar Marten (owner of Twin Oaks), and Ted Marten (leaning out of the boat, son of Oscar). William (Bill) Marten, Oscar's other son, was not swimming this day.

Six

Religion and Education

This is Amber Congregational Church in 1910. The church congregation had its beginning on August 18, 1824, when a meeting of the citizens of Amber was held at the Lake House. David Moore kept the Lake House at that time. The Amber Religious Society was organized with Dr. Killiam Lansing as clerk and Miles Bishop as chairman. Soon after, the building committee looked for a suitable site to build the church; Samuel Porter generously donated a site. The Amber Religious Society proceeded to build a church at a cost of $1,300. Approximately 60 years later, under Pastor William Briars (1884–1886), the old seats were replaced with the ones in use today. The dining room and kitchen were added in 1905–1906 and old kerosene lamps were replaced by electric lights in 1917–20.

This is a picture of Amber Church in 1917, taken in front of Bouttelle's inlet and Amber Beach.

This picture of the Amber Congregational Church was taken from an airplane in 1947. Newman's Garage is shown in the foreground. Notice how few houses were in the area.

Amber Church in 1908 had a carriage barn located on the left side of the church. Main Street in Amber, which passes in front of the church, was dirt and gravel at this time.

These notable women are members of "Scrubtown Sewing Circle of Amber Church." Pictured from left to right are Mrs. John Weeks, Sarah Hill, Mrs. Hawley, Mabel Lamb, Maree Henderson, and Adelia Tucker (teacher at Amber School). Mrs. Hawley's husband was Rev. Myron Hawley, who preached from 1924 to 1927.

The Amber Ladies Aid did volunteer work and were also called the "Amber Church House Cleaning Brigade." Pictured, from left to right, are as follows: (front row) Mrs. Hawley (pastor's wife), Sara Hill, Augusta Bishop, Ada Bishop, Marie Henderson, Della Lane, and Mae Henderson; (back row) two unidentified ladies, Frances Newman, Ida Wheeler, and Ruby Heath. They were all set to clean the church parsonage.

These are members of the Amber choir in 1940. From left to right are Carus Olcott, Myrtle Brewer, Nina Olcott, Leora Hotchkiss, Edna Bailer, Cecil Olcott, Florence Olcott, Hazel Olcott, David Olcott, and Rev. Hayes.

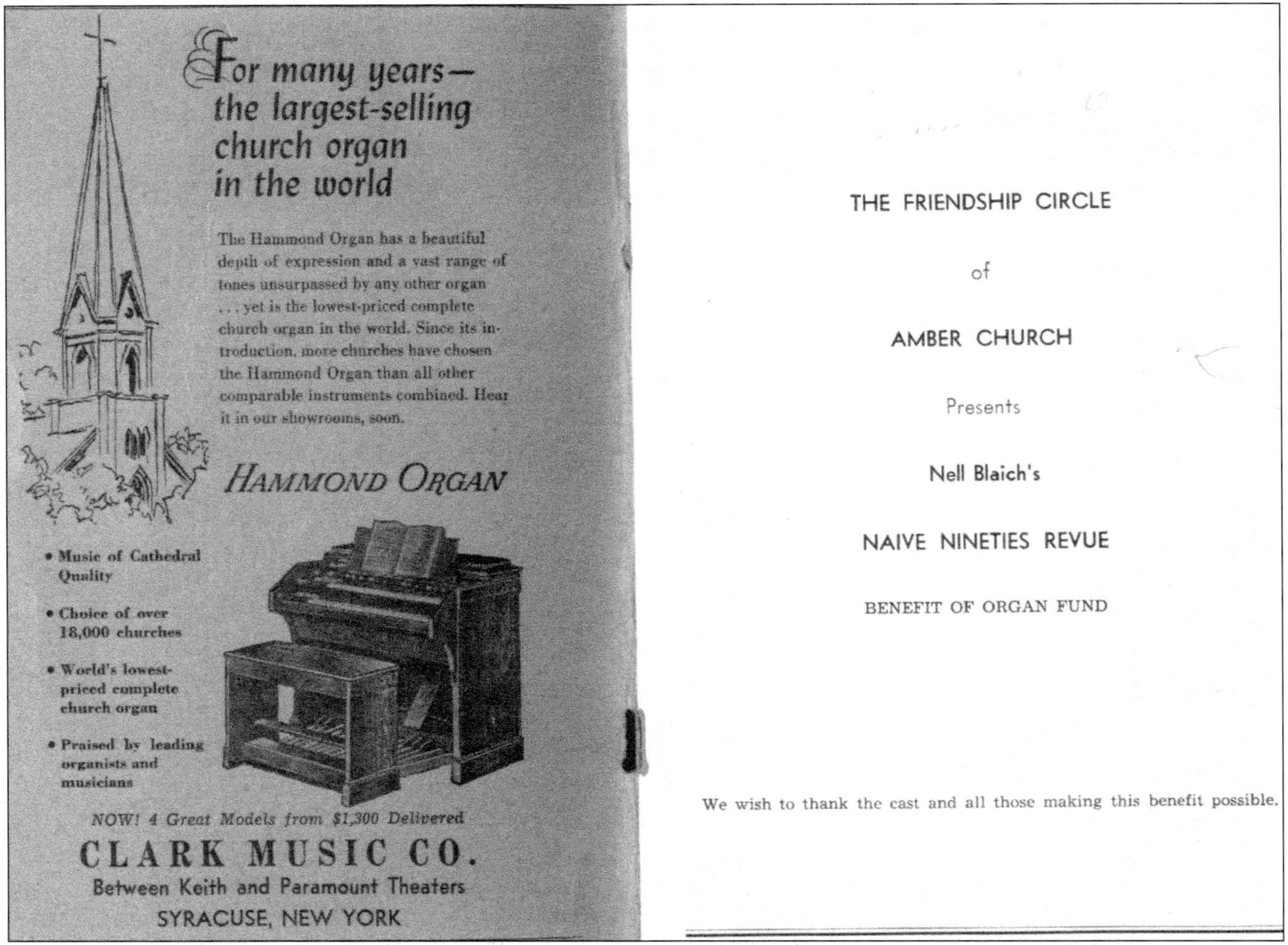

In 1949, the Amber Congregational Church needed help from the entire community to raise funds for their first organ. During the summer, the church Friendship Circle asked for help from everyone to organize and put on a show, whether they belonged to the church or not. They decided to present the *Naive Nineties Review* at the Heath's Grove Hall. They raised money for an organ similar to the one shown above. Note that this organ's price started at $1,300.

Here are members of the cast for the *Naïve Nineties Review*. Pictured, from left to right, are Mrs. Robert C. Ellis, Mrs. William F. Holihan, Mr. Holihan, and Mr. Ellis. In this photograph they are rehearsing for the performance to be presented for two evenings in Heath's Hall, Amber. Directed by Mrs. Neil Blaich, the show was sponsored by the Friendship Circle of the church. Mrs. John L. Bishop was the circle president, Mrs. Edward Wilcox and Mrs. James McBurney were the organ fund co-chairmen, and Mrs. Frank Watkins was the secretary-treasurer. The cast was comprised of local and summer residents of the community. The audience joined in the singing of gay nineties songs.

Grace and John Bishop, 1949, dressed for their role in the *Naïve Nineties Review*.

A special celebration is taking place at Amber Church in the early 1900s. With the flowers in the background and the displays on the rear walls, this event looks like Easter. However, the actual meaning of the celebration and the date are unknown. Notice the elaborate chandelier with oil lamps hanging in the middle of the church.

Rev. and Mrs. Anderson and daughter Ruth are posing for a photograph in front of the Amber Church parsonage in 1909. Both the house and barn still stand today.

After years of religious services held in homes, shops, and barns, the ladies of the community formed a corporation in 1901 called the Woman's Aid Society to build the Marietta Church. The registered members of the corporation were all women because the men said they were too busy tending to their own work. The ladies aid raised $50 through church socials and suppers and bought land from Eugene Baker. In 1903–1904, the church was built by Wright Brothers of Marcellus for $700. The bell was donated by Mr. and Mrs. George Case and the pews and chandelier donated by the Presbyterian church of Marcellus in 1906. Because the church was so small and couldn't afford much, ministers came from Auburn Seminary-Willard Chapel. Rev. William Case was the first minister. The first wedding performed in the church was for Don and Helen Hunt in November 1939. Until then, only funerals had been held here.

The oldest monuments in Amber cemetery, on the east side of the road, date back to the early 1800s. Records show that Patty Davis died and was buried in January 1815. Her grave is located at the front of the cemetery.

These photographs shows two very unique headstones in Amber cemetery. They are for Margaratha and Jacob Hoessli. Today, people stop to take photographs of these monuments since these life-like portraits are engraved in stone. Margaratha was born in 1825 and died in 1874. Jacob was born in 1812 and died in 1871.

This is Marietta School about 1910–15.

The Marietta School Class of 1920 included the following, from left to right: (front row) Elizabeth Weeks, Helen Weeks, Lyman Merrill, Dutch Burghardt, Dorothy Shea, and Catherine Hoffman; (back row) Grace Hoffman, Charlie Merrill, Edna Pople (teacher), Nelson Burleton, Emerson Miner, and Mary Burghardt.

The children of Amber School shown here include Roosevelt Curtis, Emma Heath, Ruby Smith, Irene Morgan, Donald Weeks, Bob McAvoy, Betsy Weeks, and Lyndon Bishop. Miss Tucker was one of the teachers at the time this photograph was taken in the early 1920s. The Amber School is now called the Community Center. Since the 1950s, this building has been the meeting location of the Otisco Lake Community Association. The association, as well as its predecessor organization, the Otisco Lake Civic League, sponsors activities for the community including picnics, parades, crafts, and swimming instruction.

Pictured here is the Amber School Class of 1932. Greta Grinnell is at the front left desk. Others in the class include Jane Hallas, Norma Grinnell, Emma Cook, Betsy Weeks (teacher), Roger Edinger, Betty Henderson, Louis (Dutch) Oster, J.R. Cook, Al Bishop, and Bob Negus.

The Amber School Class of 1891 or 92 is pictured here. Pictured, from left to right, are as follows: (front row) Bessie (Lamb) Harmon, Maud (Lamb) Weeks, George (Clarry) Harvard, Laura (Bishop) Vinton, Arthur Grennell, Elmer Olmstead, Henry Smith, Ernest Wheeler, Frank Morgan, and Dan Cooper; (second row) Ceylon Jackson, Stella Burroughs, Grace (Bishop) Hickman, Vicky Cooper, Etta (Bishop) Murphy, Ella (Grennell) Olmstead, Eva Beers, Clermont Jackson, Flora (Bishop) Shea, Verne Cowles, Claude Morgan, Clifford Lamb, Robert MacAvoy, and Arthur Lamb; (third row) Jesse (Jackson) Kelly, Jane (Morgan) Francisco, Bridgett Fitzgerald, Della (Tucker) Lane, Mary Fitzgerald, Ruby (Kinney) Heath, Bertha Gay, Lucy Burroughs, Fred Bishop, John Hackett, Fred Olmstead, Seth Hall, and Miles Spaulding, the teacher; (back row) Roy Redway, Orson Olmsted, and Arlo Patterson.

Oak Hill School was located at the corner of Oak Hill Road and Patterson Road, and is shown here in 1932.

Marjorie (Wheeler) Seeley taught school at the Oak Hill School during 1931 and 1932. She is a graduate of Cortland College. This photograph is from 1932. Marjorie's parents (Ernest and Mabel Wheeler) lived a quarter mile from the school. Her sister Edna was one of her students.

Pictured here is the class of 1932 at Oak Hill School. Pictured, from left to right, are as follows: (front row) David Olcott and Anita McBurney; (middle row) Merlyn McBurney, Malcolm Head, Florence Olcott, and Nina Olcott; (back row) Eugene Olcott, Carus Olcott, Lois Olcott, and Edna Wheeler. The youngster showing great individuality in the front row is David Olcott, who is currently the minister of the Rose Hill Baptist Church.

This image is of the Oak Hill School Class of 1925. Pictured, from left to right, are as follows: (front row) Raymond Wheeler, Donald Annable, Eugene Olcott, and Stanley Patterson; (back row) Gladys Patterson, Margaret Bishop, Edna Wheeler, Ethel Wheeler, Clifford Wheeler, and Reitha Head (teacher).

This was one of the classes at the Saw Mill School, located on Saw Mill Road beyond the south end of the lake. Pictured, from left to right, are as follows: (front row) Alfred Hemmings, unidentified, and Olive Rice; (second row) Bob Cates, unidentified, and Harriet Rice; (back row) Marjorie Hemmings and Nina Wilson. The teacher is Kathryn Sheehan.